W9-AJL-808

WRITING

WRITING

Blythe Camenson

VGM Career Horizons
a division of NTC Publishing Group
Lincolnwood, Illinois USA

Photo Credits:
Pages 1, 29, 43, and 57: Photo Network, Tustin, CA; pages 15 and 71: VGM photo files.
All other photographs courtesy of the author.

Library of Congress Cataloging-in-Publication Data

Camenson, Blythe.
Writing / Blythe Camenson.
p. cm. — (VGM's career portraits)
Includes index.
Summary: Introduces authorship as a career and includes information on persons who have achieved success as writers in various fields.
ISBN 0-8442-4372-8
1. Authorship—Vocational guidance—Juvenile literature. [1. Authorship—Vocational guidance. 2. Vocational guidance.] I. Title. II. Series.
PN151.C28 1996 95-19384
808'.02—dc20 CIP
AC

Published by VGM Career Horizons, a division of NTC Publishing Group
4255 West Touhy Avenue
Lincolnwood (Chicago), Illinois 60646-1975, U.S.A.

Manufactured in the United States of America.

5 6 7 8 9 0 QB 9 8 7 6 5 4 3 2 1

Contents

Of all those arts in which the wise excel,
Nature's chief masterpiece is writing well.

John Sheffield
First Duke of Buckingham and Normandy
1648–1721

Dedication

To Robyn Carr, Dana Cassell, Sarah Kennedy, Kathy Siebel, Nancy Yost, and Betty Wright, for believing in me and supporting me in my writing career.

Introduction

Although writers come from all sorts of backgrounds and no two writers are alike, they do share a few things in common. Writers love words. They love how words sound and feel and how they fit together in original and rhythmic ways.

They love playing with an idea and letting it grow into a workable article, advertisement, story, novel, or nonfiction book.

They love seeing words fill up their computer screen and print out in neat lines on what was once a blank sheet of paper.

They love the sense of accomplishment they feel when a project satisfies a client or finds a home in a book or magazine. They love seeing their name in print, and they love receiving the check, which in essence says, "Thanks for a job well done."

However, there are frustrations and disappointments, too. Becoming a professional writer is not an easy task. The new writer faces stiff competition from experienced authors, and impersonal rejection slips become a way of life. New writers sometimes must wonder if they have a better shot at winning the lottery than getting published.

But new writers do get published every year (a lot more often than anyone wins the lottery). It takes persistence, and a little luck, but if you want it more than anything else, you *can* make it happen.

This book will help you learn about all the different writing careers and how to get started. You will also meet 12 successful writers and discover how they broke into print.

Read on and decide if writing is the career for you.

WRITING FOR MAGAZINES

Visit any bookstore or newsstand and you see hundreds of magazines covering every topic from sports and cars to fashion and parenting. There are also many you won't see at the store—the hundreds of trade journals written for businesses, industries, and workers in every different career.

These publications are filled with articles, interviews, editorials, letters, advice, and dozens of advertisements. But without writers there would be nothing between the magazine covers, not even advertisements—even those are produced by writers!

The difference between staff writers and freelancers

A staff writer is employed full-time by a publication. She or he comes into work every day and receives article assignments to research and write, or works with an editor to develop ideas.

A freelance writer works independently, in rented office space or in a home office. Most freelance writers plan and write articles and columns on their own and actively seek out new markets in which to place them.

Staff writers might have less freedom in what they choose to write, but they generally have more job security and always know when their next paycheck will arrive. Freelancers trade job security and regular pay for their independence.

Both freelancers and those permanently employed have to produce high quality work. They have editors to report to and deadlines to meet.

The different kinds of articles

Articles fall into two broad categories: those that educate and those that entertain. Here is just a small sampling of typical topics for magazine articles.

- Art
- Aviation
- Business/Finance

- Careers
- Child Care
- Computers
- Contemporary Culture
- Entertainment
- Food
- Gardening
- General Interest
- Health
- Hobbies
- Military
- Nature
- Pets
- Photography
- Psychology/Self-Help
- Retirement
- Science
- Sports
- Travel

Although the subject matter can be very different, most magazine articles include many of the same elements. They all start with an interesting "hook," that first paragraph that grabs the reader's (and the editor's) attention. They use quotes from real people, mention important facts, and sometimes they include amusing anecdotes or experiences.

Before starting, read as many magazines as you can, and in particular, those you would like to write for. It's never a good idea to send an article to a magazine you have never seen before. Being familiar with the different magazines will also help you to come up with future article ideas.

Once you have decided what you want to write about, there are two ways you can proceed. You can write the entire article "on spec," send it off to appropriate editors, and hope they like your topic.

Or, you can write a query letter, a mini-proposal, to see if there is any interest in your idea first. Query letters will save you the time of writing articles you might have difficulty selling. Only once you're given a definite assignment do you then proceed.

There are three key points to keep in mind to get your articles published:

1. Make sure your writing is polished and that your article includes all the important elements.
2. Make sure your letter and manuscript are neatly typed and mistake-free.
3. Make sure you are sending your articles to the right publication. A magazine that features stories only on "Planning the Perfect Wedding" will not be interested in your piece on "Ten Tips for the Perfect Divorce."

You can find out about different magazines and the kind of material they prefer to publish in the market guides listed at the end of this chapter and throughout the book.

Most writers are thrilled to see their "byline"—that is, their name in print—giving them credit for the article. And to writers, nothing is more exciting than the finished product, getting to see their stories in print.

Getting a check or a salary for your efforts can be rewarding as well, but sadly, for new freelancers, the checks might not come often enough and are not always large enough to live on.

While staff writers are paid a regular salary (though generally not a very high one), a freelancer gets paid only when he or she sells an article. Fees could range from as low as $5 to $1,000 or more depending upon the publication. But even with a high-paying magazine, writers often have to wait until their story is published before they are paid. Because publishers work so far ahead, planning issues six months or more in advance, payment could be delayed from three months to a year or more.

To the freelancer's advantage, sometimes the same article can be sold to more than one magazine or newspaper. These "resales" help to increase salaries. And you can also be paid additional money if you can provide your own photographs to illustrate your articles.

Let's Meet...

Carol Perry
Travel Writer

Carol Perry has been a travel writer for ten years. She also writes novels for children and articles on many subjects. In addition to traveling and writing, she enjoys teaching classes on how to write travel articles.

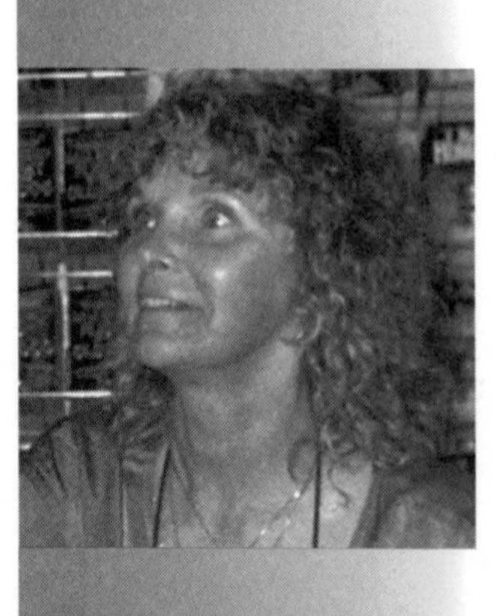

What does a travel writer do?

There are different kinds of travel articles. A service article might help readers choose luggage or give tips on traveling with pets. A destination piece takes a general look at a place, giving directions on getting there and suggesting sights to see, restaurants, and hotels. Some articles zoom in on a specific angle—such as the architecture of a district, or a famous person who lived there.

How did you get started travel writing?

I've always enjoyed traveling, and wherever I went I kept a journal and collected brochures and pamphlets from Tourist Bureaus and Chambers of Commerce. When I decided to write, the natural choice was travel writing. My first article was on side trips from London.

How do you combine travel writing with writing children's books?

I wanted to start writing books for young adults, and I wondered what setting I could use for a story. At the time, I was writing several articles on the world's largest sand castle, which was built near my home. I thought, "What a romantic place for two kids to meet." This sand castle became the background for my first young adult story, *A Sand Castle Summer*. Frequently, the travel articles I write provide material for my children's books.

What do you teach at seminars and in your classes?

I teach people how to sell their articles. I cover constructing a good query letter (a short proposal for an article that writers send to editors), submitting an article in the proper form, researching an article, getting pictures to illustrate it, and deciding where, and how often, an article can be sold.

What special qualities should a travel writer have?

Travel writers must love both travel and the written word. They must be skilled writers who understand what elements make a story interesting. Although attending college is not necessary, it's a good place to learn the basics of writing. Writers also improve their craft by attending seminars and workshops and by reading. Sometimes travel writers must also know how to take their own photographs.

"Spoking"

Generally, when writers research a travel article, they end up with enough information for more than one story. Smart writers spin off, or "spoke," other article ideas using that extra research.

The idea of "spoking" is derived from the spokes of a wheel. Below is a diagram showing how Carol Perry "spokes" several articles out of one main topic.

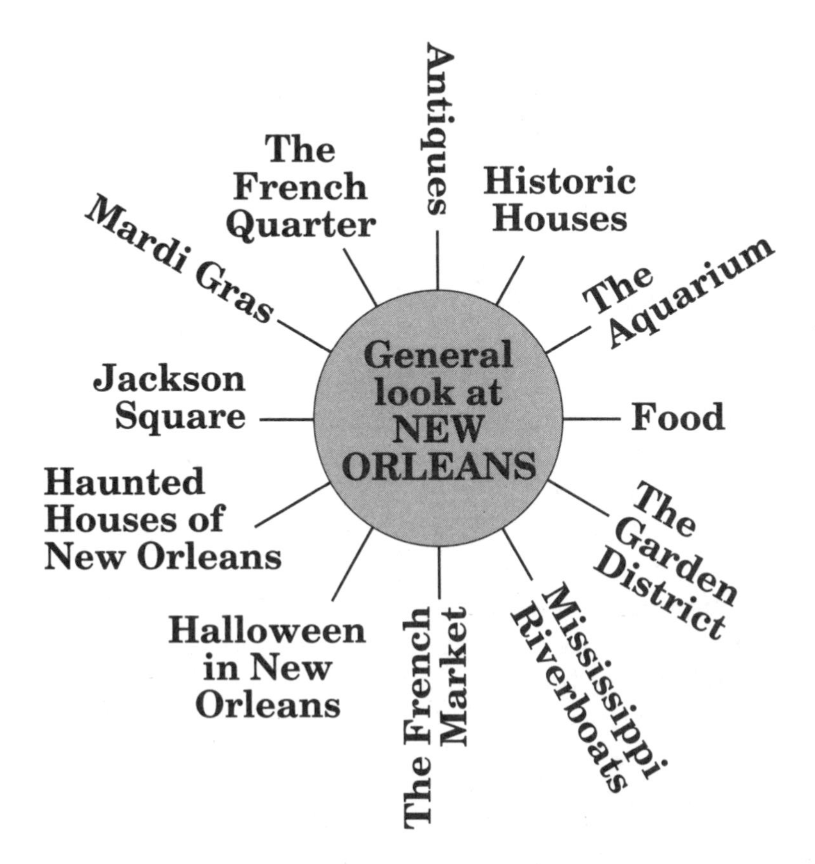

Let's Meet...

Dana Cassell has published more than 1,200 magazine articles and columns in 150+ consumer, business, and trade magazines. She is also director and founder of Cassell Network of Writers (CNW), with more than 1,000 members.

Dana Cassell

Freelance Writer

How did you get started as a writer?

Because of my high school journalism class and work on the school paper, I was able to get a job on a small-town weekly newspaper. The editor subscribed to *Writer's Digest.* I learned through this magazine that ordinary people (like me!) could write and publish articles in magazines. It opened a new world for me.

After several years of study and practice, I became a real, published freelance writer and discovered that this is what I was happiest doing.

How did CNW, Cassell Network of Writers, come about?

After working for almost 10 years, getting to know editors and other writers I met at conferences, I realized that these two groups sometimes had difficulty finding each other. That's how Cassell Network of Writers (CNW) was born. The goal of CNW is to link editors and writers and to enable writers to be more successful. I attracted 300 members the first year; membership has now grown to well over 1,000.

How would you suggest someone get started writing for magazines?

Not going to college didn't make much difference for me, but nowadays you need a degree to get a staff job on a magazine or newspaper (which is a good way to learn the ropes for freelancing). And a college degree, with business courses, will prevent mistakes. I don't think going to college guarantees success, but if you combine being a self-starter with a formal education, you can probably be successful, faster, easier.

Take any high school or college journalism classes available; work on the school paper; take marketing, advertising, and business classes; learn to type and word process.

Read books and magazines targeted to the small businessperson and the writer to better learn about the problems and pitfalls.

What do you like most about your work?

I love the freedom of being my own boss; the excuse to talk to anybody about anything while doing research; the continual use of books, magazines, and libraries; the ability to work at home; seeing my byline; and the satisfaction that information I provide helps writers become successful.

Nothing equals the excitement of coming up with an idea for an article or book, following it through, and having someone publish it.

Dana's Busy Schedule

8:00–8:15:	Filed reference material.
8:15–10:00:	Worked on my book manuscript.
10:00–10:20:	Went to the post office.
10:20–11:00:	Opened & sorted mail, logged in income.
11:00–2:30:	Ran errands.
2:30–3:00:	Returned phone calls.
3:00–4:30:	Skimmed a few magazines, brainstormed ideas for new articles.
4:30–5:30:	Cooked and ate dinner.
5:30–5:45:	Worked on computer mailing list.
5:45–6:45:	Worked on a writing project.
6:45–7:15:	Worked on a marketing plan for my books.
7:15–7:45:	Updated information on the computer.
7:45–8:40:	Printed out mailing labels for state conference. Cataloged personal CD collection.
8:40–9:15:	Installed a new software program.
9:15–9:30:	Planned next day's tasks.

Here are the requirements of two national magazines. Be aware that these publications are difficult for beginners to break into, but if you are familiar with the magazines and have practiced your writing skills, you may be one of the lucky ones.

publishes articles, short stories, and poetry aimed at young women ages 12 to 20. Pays $50 to $150 for articles written by teenagers (pays more to adults). Send brief outline with your query. Include the first paragraph of the article that sums up the basic idea. Send to Editor, *Seventeen Magazine,* 850 3rd Ave., New York, NY 10022. Before submitting, write and request their guidelines for writers. Don't forget your SASE (self-addressed stamped envelope).

publishes fiction, nonfiction, poetry, activities, and book-related features for children 8 to 11. They usually only buy fiction from well-known children's authors, but give it a try. Freelancers have a better chance with nonfiction articles about children involved in interesting activities related to books, reading, or writing. Pays $150 per published magazine page upon acceptance. Send a query letter with article ideas and writing samples. Story length is no longer than 800 words. Contact Tamara Hanneman, Editor, *Storyworks*, Scholastic, Inc., 555 Broadway, New York, NY 10012.

Find Out More

Every career has its own language, and writing and publishing are no exception. Here are some terms you will find throughout this book.

Advance: Money a publisher pays to a writer who is working on a book.

Byline: Your name in print on an article you wrote.

Contract: Legal agreement between a writer and a publisher or agent.

Copy: The words in an ad or on a book cover, for example.

Fiction: Any work that is imaginary, made up by the author.

Guidelines: An information sheet writers can request from publishers. It explains what to submit and how to submit it.

Market: As a verb, to market means to sell your work. As a noun, market means the place—the publisher, magazine, newspaper—where you can sell your work, or the audience for your work.

Nonfiction: Work that is true, factual.

Proposal: A written presentation for a book or article idea.

Query Letter: A mini-proposal for a book or article in the form of a letter.

SASE: Self-addressed, stamped envelope. Send an SASE with every submission.

Slush Pile: Unsolicited manuscripts at an agency or publishing house. They pile up until someone has time to read them.

Submission: Manuscript or query letter sent to an editor or agent for consideration.

Synopsis: A written summary of your novel's plot.

Unsolicited Submission: A manuscript you send in without being invited to submit.

For more information about writing for magazines:

Society of American Travel Writers
1155 Connecticut Avenue
Suite 500
Washington, D.C. 20006

How to Write Irresistible Query Letters, by Lisa Collier Cool, Writer's Digest Books, 1987. Everything you need to know to get an editor's attention and successfully sell your articles.

Market Guide for Young Writers, Writer's Digest Books. Lots of good advice for young writers from ages 8 through 18, including tips on getting started, listings of buyers, how to submit material, payments, writing contests, and prizes.

WRITING FOR NEWSPAPERS

Do you like being on top of things, always knowing what's going on around you? If so, working for a newspaper might be the career for you. Reporters, editors, and photojournalists cover every story—from crime to fashion.

An adventurous reporter might relish the idea of being in the thick of a riot or chasing fire engines to the scene of a car wreck. For the more sedate, there are specialized fields to cover such as health, fashion, food or entertainment.

This chapter describes the world of newspapers, the different jobs and assignments, and how journalists bring us the news.

Some newspapers are large city dailies; others are small-town weeklies. Whatever the size or location, the job of newspaper writers is to cover local, state, national, and international events and put all this news together to keep the reading public informed.

Reporters gather information by visiting the scene, interviewing people, following leads, and examining documents. While some reporters might rely on their memory, most take notes or use a tape recorder while collecting facts. Back in the office, they organize their material, choose the focus, and write their stories.

Because of deadlines, many reporters use portable computers to file the story while away from the office. The story is then sent by telephone modem directly to the newspaper's computer system.

The departments within newspapers vary from location to location, but most include some, if not all, of the following sections:

- Art/Entertainment
- Books
- Business
- Consumer Affairs
- Crime Desk
- Education
- Fashion
- Finance
- Food
- Foreign Affairs
- Health
- International News
- Lifestyles/Features
- Local News
- National News
- Religion
- Science
- Social Events
- Sports
- State News
- Travel
- Weather

Some newspapers have modern, state-of-the-art equipment; others do not. A reporter could work in a comfortable, private office, or in a room filled with the noise of computer printers or co-workers talking on the telephone.

Working hours vary. Some writers and editors work Monday through Friday, nine to five; others cover evenings, nights, and weekends. On some occasions, reporters work longer than normal hours to cover a late-breaking or ongoing story.

A college degree is a must; most employers prefer a B.A. in journalism, while others would accept a degree in a related field such as political science or English. In high school you can concentrate on English and journalism courses, as well as social studies and computer science.

Previous work on a school paper or an internship at a newspaper will help improve your resume. Experience as a "stringer"—a part-time reporter paid only for stories printed—is also helpful.

Jobs at newspapers are expected to grow in the next 10 years, especially with the small town and suburban dailies and weeklies. But competition for jobs on the large urban newspapers will continue to be fierce. Editors prefer to hire top graduates from accredited programs. A beginning reporter would probably have better luck starting out at a small paper, gaining a year or so of experience, and then moving on. Reporters must be prepared to move to find the right job.

While on the job, be on the lookout for a mentor. Look to someone who is older, more experienced, someone you can trust and who will take your career seriously. A mentor can answer questions and help analyze mistakes so you don't repeat them.

The Newspaper Guild negotiates reporters' wages with newspapers, both the starting minimum salary and the top minimum, which takes effect after 3 to 6 years of employment. Salaries vary depending upon the region of the country in which you work. Some cities, such as New York and Washington, pay high wages, but the cost of living there is also much higher.

A beginning reporter at a small paper could start at about $15,000 a year. In a big city, a reporter could start with a salary of $25,000 or so. The average top minimum salary for a reporter with a few years' experience is about $34,000 a year.

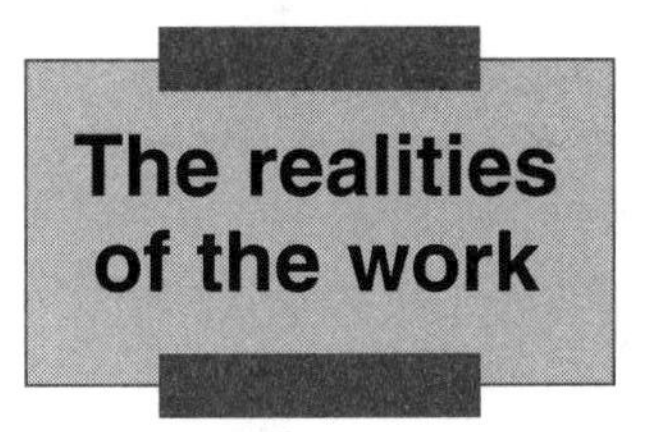

Reporters, photojournalists, and editors always have deadlines to meet. Unlike fiction writers, who can work at their own pace, reporters do not have the luxury of waiting for their creative juices to flow. A news reporter has to file a story, or maybe even two, every day by a certain time. A writer with a weekly column has more leeway, but still, everything must be in on time.

A reporter also must know how to "write tight." While feature writers can be more creative, news reporters must make all the facts fit—the who, what, when, where, why, and how—within a certain space.

Let's Meet...

Michael Malone received his bachelor's degree in photojournalism at San Jose State University in California in 1981. He is assistant director of photography at a major newspaper.

Michael Malone

Photojournalist

Can you give us a definition of photojournalism?

Photojournalism is telling a story through pictures. And although the photographs dominate over written copy, photojournalists need to have a strong journalism background, too. To report the news, you should have a complete understanding of the subject, and you need to be aware of what's happening in the world. You could cover exciting stories, in a war zone, for example, where there's a lot of peril. But being a Jack-of-all-trades is the main requirement. Most photojournalists, for both major and minor newspapers, are expected to cover tamer stories, too. The gamut runs from food, to fashion, to spot news, to sports, to a wide range of human interest features.

What kind of training should future photojournalists have?

Photojournalism is highly competitive, so having a good education is very important. You have to work hard, get good grades, make contacts, and be 100 percent committed to your career. Most photojournalists have at least a bachelor's degree; many, especially those with management inclinations, have a master's.

How would someone go about finding a job in photojournalism?

There are different routes to take in the job-hunting process, but they all include putting together a professional portfolio.

Some photojournalists identify papers they would like to work for, and, at their own expense, fly out to talk to the different editors—even when they know there are currently no openings. This approach, though a bit costly for someone just starting out, often works. When an opening does occur, potential employers will remember your eager smile and top-quality portfolio.

But I think job hunting through the mail is just as effective. Send out your portfolio with a good cover letter, and don't be afraid to mention any story ideas you might have. Newspapers aren't looking for robots; they appreciate a photojournalist who does more than stand behind the camera and click the shutter.

Then follow up about a week later as a reminder. I've made up my own picture postcards, using my best work. This helps to jog the editor's memory—and shows how creative you are.

Another successful method is to take more than the one required college internship. If you can get extra internships, you'll make more contacts and have a better chance of lining up full-time employment.

A View of Hurricane Andrew

Being from California, Michael was used to natural disasters such as earthquakes, but, he said, "the idea of living through a hurricane was something I found terrifying as well as intriguing."

He spent the night of the hurricane at his newspaper's headquarters in Fort Lauderdale; then at about six in the morning he went out to view the damage. "I thought I had seen Mother Nature's wrath before with earthquake damage, but nothing had prepared me for this."

As he traveled south the destruction worsened. "Coming across boats sitting in the middle of the street, and visiting where the brunt of the hurricane had hit, seeing all that damage from the force of the wind—as both a citizen and a photojournalist, it was a powerful experience. It's nothing I'm in a hurry to experience again, but it was pretty amazing."

Let's Meet...

Rod Stafford Hagwood

Fashion Editor

Rod earned his bachelor's degree in broadcast journalism from Memphis State University. He started freelance writing in college, and in 1990 began his present job as fashion editor.

How did you get started in your career?

It was not any great career plan. My guidance counselor in high school suggested I consider law, maybe because my father was an attorney, but it didn't interest me. Too many rules. I was interested in writing, though I didn't really know what to do to make a living out of it.

I started freelancing for local papers while I was in college, writing entertainment. I got lucky and met some people who helped arrange interviews I normally wouldn't have been able to get. For example, I got to interview Tom Cruise, right before "Top Gun" came out. And Emilio Estevez, Molly Ringwald, and George Michael.

By the time I graduated, for someone who didn't have a plan, I already had an impressive portfolio. I also had a job offer with Gannett, the parent company of a lot of newspapers, including *USA*

Today. They said I could intern at one of their papers and that I'd have a full-time job when I finished.

I interned at the *Arkansas Gazette*. Again, Fate put me in the right place. While getting involved in fund-raisers in Little Rock, I met Mr. and Mrs. Clinton. I wrote about them constantly. I got to write about everything: classical music, fashion, society pieces. I did everything from flying with the Blue Angels to attending debutante balls in restricted country clubs.

What are your duties as fashion editor?

My main duty is to produce the Sunday fashion page. That means making sure the art is up to the art department's standards, making sure the photography is up to the photography department's standards, and making sure the layout artist gets all the different elements in plenty of time.

Then there's the writing. I have to make sure the articles are written, which involves phone calls and research. It doesn't just come tripping off the tongue as people think.

What do you like most about your job?

The ability to define my own rules. If I'm interested in something, I can go find out about it. Last week I told my editor I was going to the beach to see what people are wearing when they step off the sand, and she didn't even bat an eye. That's the fun part of the job. If something catches your eye, you can go investigate it.

From Intern to Editor

Even though Rod already had a firm offer with Gannett, he wasn't sure where he wanted to work. Then he heard of an opening at a paper in Fort Lauderdale, Florida. The job was as fashion editor.

"To be honest, I was more interested in spending a weekend in Florida than I was in the interview. I already had a job offer.

"At the interview they asked what I would do as the fashion editor. I hadn't taken the job offer very seriously, so I didn't have specific plans. Instead I told them the kind of section I would want to write no matter where I was. I wanted it to be something whimsical that didn't take itself seriously. I wanted it to be a little naughty, too, so people would say, 'Oh, there he goes again.'

"And I wanted the fashion page to have a distinctive voice, that people would instantly recognize. They responded well to my answer and made me a very pleasant offer.

"This was about five and a half years ago. A fashion editor who worked for Reuters said to me, 'That area is it, that's next. Whatever is going to happen in fashion is going to happen in South Beach.'

"I took her advice and here I am. South Beach exploded onto the world stage, and I moved straight from an internship into an editor's job."

Dave Barry writes a humor column for the *Miami Herald,* his hometown paper. But as happens to one in a billion people, other newspapers across the country found out about him, and they pay him every week to print his column.

Pulitzer found out about him and gave him a big cash prize to reward his good sense of humor.

Hollywood found out about him and created "Dave's World," a TV show based loosely on his life. ("Very loosely," Dave says. "Harry Anderson is a lot taller than me.")

Even Stephen King found out about him and, together with author Amy Tan and other notables, they loosely play in a rock and roll band called The Rock Bottom Remainders. ("Very loosely," Dave says. "We only know the words to *Louie, Louie.*")

Dave has written several books, among them: *Dave Barry Turns 40, Dave Barry Talks Back, Dave Barry Does Japan,* and his newest, *Dave Barry Is Not Making This Up.*

What does he write about? Very important topics that affect all of us. Exploding Pop-Tarts, for example. And the World's Fastest Lawn Mower. And bad songs and lyrics like "MacArthur Park" where a cake was left out in the rain, and "Careless Whisper"—"I'm never gonna dance again; guilty feet have got no rhythm." And don't forget this classic, "Ain't No Woman Like the One-Eyed Gott."

How does Dave explain the secret to his success? "I have always kept one vital journalistic principle foremost in my mind: *Try not to leave the house.*"

Find Out More

Take this mini-quiz to see if journalism is the right career for you. Answer *True* or *False*.

	TRUE	FALSE
1. You have a favorite city and a favorite newspaper in mind and you will only consider working there.	___	___
2. You expect to be paid a good salary and to work normal hours.	___	___
3. You don't know how to type, but you figure you'll learn while on the job.	___	___
4. Your writing teachers suggested you try to write "tighter."	___	___
5. When you start your new job, you expect to be given the exciting assignments you've always dreamed of.	___	___

Answers: If you answered *False* to *all* of the above questions, then a career in journalism might just be the right choice for you.

To find out more, contact the following associations.

American Newspaper Publishers Association Foundation
The Newspaper Center
Box 17407
Dulles International Airport
Washington, DC 20041
The association has career information including these pamphlets: *Newspapers: What's In It For Me?* and *Facts about Newspapers.*

The Dow Jones Newspaper Fund
P.O. Box 300
Princeton, NJ 08543-0300

National Newspaper Association
1627 K St., NW, Suite 400
Washington, DC 20006

National Press Photographers Association (NPPA)
3200 Cloasdaile Drive, Suite 306
Durham, NC 27705

Fiction writers are imaginative people. Whether they write short stories or full-length novels, fiction writers have to be able to create imaginary characters and events and make them seem real to their readers.

Fiction writers have to be troublemakers, too, inventing all sorts of problems for their characters. They have to make fictional conversations and thoughts entertaining, and fill their characters' lives with action. Finally, fiction writers have to be expert problem solvers, helping their heroes find satisfying solutions to their troubles by the end of the story.

If you love to read fiction and want to create imaginary worlds of your own, read on. This chapter explains the ups and downs of writing fiction and getting it published.

Few new fiction writers have the luxury of working at their craft full-time. Most need another job to help pay the bills until they can support themselves through their writing. Dedicated writers use every spare minute they have to work on their books or stories. John Grisham, for example, wrote a good deal of *The Firm* while taking the train to and from his job as a full-time attorney.

Others get up earlier, stay up later, turn down invitations to social events, or let the housework go—whatever they can do to find the time to write.

Successful authors who support themselves through their writing treat it as a full-time job. Most discipline themselves to put in a certain number of hours each day. Every writer chooses a schedule that is comfortable for him or her. Some work in the early morning, take afternoon naps, then go back to the computer in the evenings. Others write for eight to twelve hours straight each day for months until the book is finished. Still others take years to complete one volume.

There is no set formula for how a writer should work. The only rule is that you have to write. Author James Clavell said that even if you write only one page every day for a year, at the end of that time you'll have 365 pages. And that's a good-size book.

Writing a short story or novel is only half the battle. In addition to becoming an expert storyteller, you also have to become a knowledgeable salesperson. You must learn which publishers you should approach, and how to approach them. There are several market guides, which are mentioned at the end of this chapter, that will tell you what categories of fiction the different publishers buy. The guides also list the different magazines that purchase short stories. You can also check your own book collection to learn about publishers.

Once you've made a list of possible markets, you need to make sure your approach is appropriate. Your manuscript needs to be typed and double-spaced, with your name at the top of each page. Several sources can give you the information you need to format your manuscript properly.

Before you send in your completed manuscript, write the editor a brief letter describing your project. Include a one-page synopsis, or summary of your book's plot, and the first three chapters of your book as a sample. Don't forget to enclose an SASE, a self-addressed stamped envelope. The editor will use this to send you a reply. If the editor likes your first submission, you'll probably receive a request to send more.

Alternatively, you can look for an agent first, following the same steps you'd use to approach a publisher. But this time, you are asking that the agent consider you as a possible client.

At this point, after the query letters and sample chapters are in the mail, many new writers just sit back and wait for responses. The smart writers put that manuscript out of their heads and get to work on the next one. And the next one.

In the end, the key to getting published can be summed up in one word: persistence.

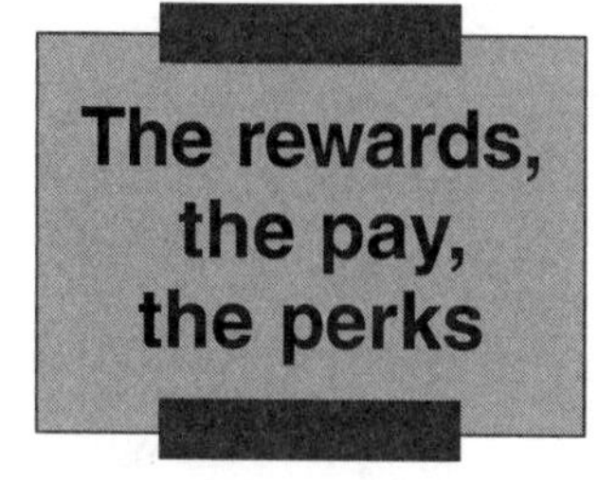

"Don't give up your day job just yet," is what the experts advise. Even if you sell your first novel, you would expect to receive only about $2,500 or $5,000. The six-figure advances that some superstar authors receive are not the norm. Zebra Books senior editor John Scognamiglio (see his interview in the section on Careers in Publishing) says, "That kind of stuff like with John Grisham doesn't really have anything to do with the rest of us. There are 110,000 new titles a year and only 15 are on the *NY Times Bestseller List* at a time. Most of us make a moderate income and do a civilized business if we work very, very hard."

If you do manage to land that first book contract, you probably will receive an advance against royalties. A royalty is a percentage, usually 6 to 10 percent, of the money your book earns in sales. The advance is paid half on signing the contract, half on delivery and acceptance of the manuscript.

But money is not the only reason writers write. For some, the profession is almost an obsession—a burning desire to put words to paper, to start a book and see it to its finish. They wouldn't be happy doing anything else. Other perks include recognition and publicity, though some might view the attention as a downside. Many writers report that the nicest perk is being able to go to work in their bathrobe.

Let's Meet...

Robyn Carr

Novelist

Robyn Carr has written 14 novels since 1980. Her latest book, *Mind Tryst,* is a psychological thriller. Robyn also taught for The Writer's Digest School of Writing and wrote *Practical Tips for Writing Popular Fiction* (Writer's Digest Books).

How did you get started in writing?

I read a lot and thought anybody with half a brain could write, which is how everyone thinks in the beginning. You're sure your first book is *Gone With the Wind,* but it's really junk. But something happens to you when you're doing it. I developed an obsessive desire to write.

How do you construct your plots?

With romance I just use notes and simple 1, 2, 3, a, b, c outlines. But in suspense so much rests on when certain discoveries are made. I have to make plot outlines on index cards so that I can lay them out on the table and move them around. For example, when will Jackie discover things about Tom Wall (lead characters in *Mind Tryst*)? Or when does Jackie use the gun? How these elements are arranged throughout the book is important to the reader.

How do you keep readers turning the pages?

A classic mistake made by new writers, which I made many times, is confusing building suspense with withholding information. Actually, the more information you give, the more suspense you build.

Another problem with keeping secrets is that it breaks a hard-and-fast rule. If your main character, from whose viewpoint the story is written, knows something, the reader also has to know it. The information can be kept secret from other characters, but the reader is in the main character's head, and the character can't hide her thoughts from the reader.

The first rule of mystery is that your readers are entitled to an equal opportunity with your characters to solve the mystery.

Tell us about the writing process.

I was at a writer's conference, and someone asked, "Should you force yourself to write a book from beginning to end, should you outline first, should you revise as you go along?" Everyone on the panel of six successful published authors said that you should outline first, force yourself to write through, and then revise. However, I keep getting stuck going back to the beginning and revising before I can carry on.

I have a real clear idea before I begin what's going to happen. Some minor things change but the basic premise—who the bad guy is and how it's going to end—is real solid.

Robyn's First Sale

My first agent lived in San Antonio. He'd just opened the agency and was trying to build it up. He was my fourth or fifth attempt. I had been submitting things on my own before. I wrote query letters and killed myself hammering out synopses and revising the first three chapters four hundred times. I would get the envelope ready for the next submission before the rejection came so I wouldn't be paralyzed with grief.

My agent made multiple copies and sent it to 13 publishers—the 13th publisher took it. Avon, Bantam, and Berkley rejected it, and my heart was sinking lower and lower. I knew there was no hope; then Little Brown & Company finally bought it, and I said, "Little who?" They are one of the finest publishers in America, but I hadn't heard of them.

My first novel, *Chelynne,* was published in 1980.

Let's Meet...

Joyce Sweeney started sending her work to publishers when she was just 8 years old. She sold her first book when she was 18. Now, 8 books later, Joyce still loves writing about adolescents.

Joyce Sweeney

Young Adult Writer

How did you get started writing?

I knew I wanted to be a writer all my life. I started writing when I was a kid, about other kids. But I didn't know that the Young Adult genre existed.

I would look through magazines to find the editors' addresses and send them a poem. I was used to rejections by the time I was a teenager. I didn't really know what I was doing, but the whole process made me feel good.

Later, miraculously, I found an agent. She submitted *Center Line* to more than 30 publishers. I was nervous, but I knew it was a good book. Then Delacorte Press held a contest for new authors, and I won first place. The prize was $5,000 and publication. Delacorte is now my publisher.

What do you write about?

Whatever interests me at the moment. My readers are 10- to 14-year-olds. My book *Shadow* is a ghost story, but it's also about sibling rivalry and domestic violence. Another book is an adventure story about four boys trapped in a cave.

What do you like most about writing for children?

They're a more appreciative audience than adults. I go to schools, and I find I have real fans. They're excited and enthusiastic; they write letters to me. I think back to when I was a kid, and I know that the books they read at that age make a huge difference. It's exciting to be able to influence them.

Are there any downsides?

I find it a little difficult to market myself. At a children's event, the kids there are too young for my books. At an event with adult authors, no one is really interested.

And just being a writer is a constant struggle. It's difficult to write; it's difficult to keep writing. You know you could make more money in advertising.

I've started books and found they were going nowhere and had to throw them out. I haven't had many bad reviews, but I've had books that I thought were great that didn't sell that well. There are ups and downs all the time. There's the unpredictability of sales and whether the next book will be as good as the one before it.

What's your advice for aspiring writers?

Read as much as you possibly can, and read the authors you would like to be like. Enroll in creative writing classes. And no matter how young you are, send things out, for the practice and to get used to rejection slips.

Books by Joyce Sweeney

Center Line: After the death of their mother, five brothers are left to live with an alcoholic, abusive father. They run away and spend a year on the road, learning how tough it can be out on their own.

Right Behind the Rain: Twenty-year-old Kevin is a dancer with a successful career on its way, but he begins to feel the pressure of his family's expectations. He becomes seriously depressed, and his little sister is the only one who recognizes the trouble he's in.

Dream Collector: A family decides that each member should make a wish on Christmas Eve. They spend the next year making those wishes come true, but only one person ends up happy.

Face the Dragon: Six kids in a gifted program in high school read *Beowulf* and decide to face their own personal problems.

Piano Man: A fourteen-year-old girl develops an obsessive crush on a twenty-year-old neighbor and soon she's lost in a fantasy world.

The Tiger Orchard: Eighteen-year-old Zack sees a psychiatrist because he's having nightmares. He finds out that his nightmares are really old memories from his childhood and that the father he thought was dead is still alive.

Shadow: A young girl believes her dead cat has returned as a ghost. A psychic housekeeper is convinced the cat is trying to help a family member in trouble.

John Grisham is an attorney turned writer. With six books in print (*A Time to Kill, The Firm, The Pelican Brief, The Client, The Chamber, The Rainmaker*), several of which have been made into feature films, he commands very impressive advances. His first four books set a record by being on the best-seller list all at the same time.

But success didn't come quickly, or easily. First Grisham had difficulty finding an agent to take him on; then it took his agent a year to sell Grisham's first novel. A slew of rejection notices was finally replaced by the all-important acceptance—handed to him by Bill Thompson, an editor who is not afraid of promoting a newcomer. (He was the one who gave Stephen King his chance when no one else would, and published his first novel, *Carrie.*) Thompson paid Grisham $15,000 for *A Time to Kill.* It came out in June, 1989, with a print run of 5,000. "I bought 1,000, and another 1,000 were sitting in a warehouse, so you know not many were out there," said Grisham in an interview in *Publishers Weekly.*

Events progressed more rapidly with his second book, *The Firm.* A bootleg copy of his manuscript landed in the hands of Hollywood, and Paramount paid Grisham $600,000 for the movie rights. And this was before a publisher had even seen the manuscript.

There are now more than 20 million copies of his books in print.

Advice for New Writers

Here are several pieces of advice for new writers:

1. Read, read, and read some more. It's important to read other writers, and to know what other people are reading. The best writers are avid readers.
2. Write the kind of book you like to read.
3. Find someone to read your work. It's difficult for writers to distance themselves enough, and someone else might find something you might have missed.
4. Don't be afraid of criticism; part of writing is rejection.
5. Don't get too attached to your words. All writers must constantly rewrite.
6. Whatever you submit should be professionally presented. It should be neatly typed, with margins, and you should include a nice cover letter. The presentation is what catches an editor's or agent's eye.
7. Keep writing. Don't ever stop trying to perfect your skills.
8. Don't give up. If you keep at it, you'll eventually find a home for your work.

Find out more about fiction writing

American Society of Journalists and Authors
1501 Broadway
New York, NY 10036

These guides, published by Writer's Digest Books, will show you where and how to submit your work.

Guide To Literary Agents & Art/Photo Reps. In addition to 500+ listings of agents and what they handle, this annual guide showcases articles of interest to writers.

Novel & Short Story Writer's Market. This annual guide provides more than 1,900 entries of fiction-publishing opportunities including big publishers, small presses, consumer and literary magazines. The guide also offers advice and inspiration from top editors and authors.

Children's Writer's and Illustrator's Market. This annual guide can help aspiring writers and artists to make sure their submissions end up on the right desk. Contains nearly 700 markets including children's book publishers, magazines, scriptwriting markets, greeting card companies, and markets for writing and artwork *by* children.

WRITING NONFICTION BOOKS

Nonfiction titles published each year outnumber fiction titles by more than two to one. This means twice as many opportunities for the beginning nonfiction book writer. In fact, most competent writers can find a home for their work.

But a nonfiction writer needs to be an expert in a specialized field of knowledge, right?

Wrong. A nonfiction book writer doesn't have to start out as an expert, though he or she may become one by the time the book is finished. In this chapter you will learn how to gather the information you need to propose, write, and publish your nonfiction book.

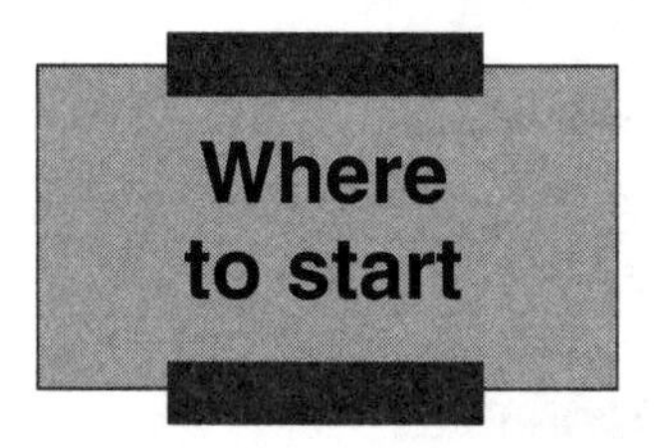

As with any book, you must start with an idea, a topic that interests you. Nonfiction authors write about everything under the sun. Here is just a small sampling of general categories that interest publishers.

- Autobiography
- Biography
- Career/Finding a Job
- Childcare
- Cooking
- Dieting
- Health/Fitness
- History
- Hobbies
- How-To
- Investing and Making Money
- New Age
- Parenting
- Relationships
- Self-Help/Psychology
- Spiritual
- Textbooks
- Travel

At this writing, among the current top 15 best-selling nonfiction books there are 3 autobiographies, 2 biographies, 1 cookbook, 1 fitness, 1 history, 2 politics, 1 relationship, and 4 spiritual/New Age.

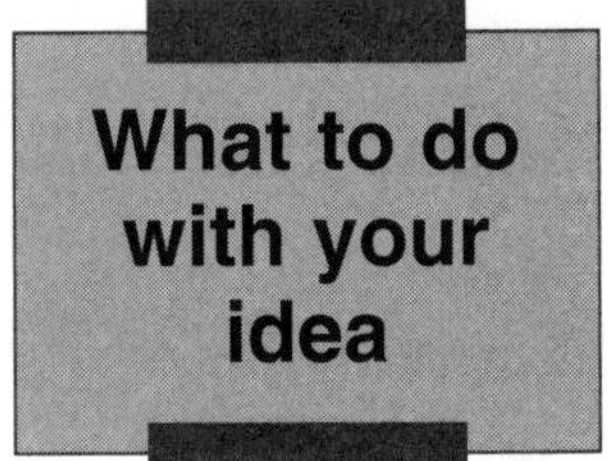

First, check what's already been written on the subject. You won't get your book published if it duplicates the information of a hundred other books. However, if your book will add to the information currently available—in other words, if your book will fill a gap in the marketplace—then you have a shot at getting it published.

Go to the library and the bookstore and see what's already out there. Note the publishers because they might be the ones who will be interested in your book, too. Once you have examined the competing books, you can decide if your idea is still a good one.

Before you write your proposal, which is your entry into a literary agency or a publishing house, you have to make sure you can collect the information you will need to write your book.

If you already are an expert in a particular area, you have a head start. But you still will need facts to complete your book. Most nonfiction writers use two sources for information: books, articles, and documents on the subject; and interviews with professionals or experts in the field. If you are writing a biography of a famous person, for example, you can study other books written about that person's life, and you can track down and interview people who know that person.

After you've done your initial research—you have your idea, you know what the competition is, and you know how to gather the information you'll need to write the book—you are ready to compose a query letter. This is a mini-proposal, telling an editor or agent about your book idea: why you think it should be published, who the readers will be, and why you are the best person to write this book. You end your letter by offering to send a full proposal and sample chapters.

The proposal is a longer version of your query letter. It should include a table of contents that shows you know how to organize the material for your book, and one or two sample chapters. If the editor or agent likes your proposal, he or she will probably ask to see the completed manuscript. Few first-time writers can land a book contract without a finished book, but sometimes a good proposal can get you a sale.

Your proposal could also save you the time of writing a book that will never get published. You might learn from the editors or agents that there is no interest in your idea for a number of reasons. Here are some possibilities:

1. There are too many similar books on the same subject.
2. Earlier books on the subject did not sell well.
3. The audience for your book is too narrow—not enough people would be interested in it.
4. Your book doesn't cover enough ground.
5. Your book covers too much ground.

If your book idea should be turned down, don't get discouraged. The feedback you get from agents and editors can give you an idea about how to revise your book, or might lead you to a new topic.

If you do receive that exciting phone call or letter informing you your book has been accepted, you can expect to receive a book contract that will spell out all the terms. An advance for a nonfiction book could be from $1,000 on up, to even a million dollars or more, depending on how big the publishing house is, how timely and important your book topic is, and how many books the publishers believe they'll be able to sell. First-time writers should expect to fall somewhere at the bottom of the scale. You will also be paid royalties, a percentage of the price of each book that sells.

Let's Meet...

Jim Haskins is a distinguished author with 101 published books to his credit, one of which is *The Cotton Club,* the book that inspired the movie. His interests include biography, music, history, and language. He is also a university professor.

Jim Haskins

Biographer

Tell us how you got started.

I just fell into it. I didn't grow up thinking I wanted to be a writer. My first book wasn't really a book; it was my diary—*Diary of a Harlem Schoolteacher*. It ended up being a book because I knew someone who worked in publishing. She had a look and saw its potential.

How do you research your biographies?

If the subjects are agreeable, I'll interview them. In some cases when they won't do it, their family and friends talk to me. For example, with Michael Jackson, I talked to his brothers. I don't think even Barbara Walters could talk to Michael Jackson.

How long does it take to write a book?

It depends on the book, how long it is, and what audience it's for. *Scott Joplin* took seven years; another took three. I've been working on another book for 20 years. There's really no rule of thumb; I could write some books in three weeks.

How do you schedule your time?

I write in hotels and on airplanes and everywhere else. I don't use computers; I can't think on them. I write in longhand on yellow legal pads; then I type up the manuscript on an old Royal manual. Then someone enters it into the computer for me.

For me writing is a job and a craft. There's nothing particularly romantic about it. Some days I don't write at all. I have to do a lot of reading and research before I sit down and write. Some days I read, some days I think about what I want to write, and then when it comes, it comes. I'll sit and do it. That could be two or three o'clock in the morning.

What do you like most about your work?

I like that I have the leisure to do it. Reading and writing is a luxury of the leisure class. You can't be a writer unless you're a reader. And you can't be a reader unless you have the time.

What accomplishments are you most proud of?

The fact that *The Cotton Club* was the first book ever optioned for a movie by a Black person in America was important, I think. The book was a big seller. And my book on Scott Joplin was made into a movie for television.

And the fact that I wrote the first book on a number of people: Ella Fitzgerald, Scott Joplin, Scatman, Nat King Cole.

A List To Be Proud Of

Many of Jim's books are of interest to young people. Although 101 are too many to mention here, below is a selected list of his books. You can find them in bookstores or at your local library.

About Michael Jackson

Amazing Grace: The Story Behind the Song

Bill Cosby: America's Most Famous Father

Breakdancing

Christopher Columbus: Admiral of the Ocean Sea

Colin Powell

The Cotton Club

Diary of a Harlem Schoolteacher

Ella Fitzgerald: A Life Through Jazz

I Am Somebody! A Biography of Jesse Jackson

The Life and Death of Martin Luther King, Jr.

Richard Pryor: A Man and His Madness

Scott Joplin: The Man Who Made Ragtime (coauthored with Kathleen Benson)

Shirley Temple Black: Actress to Ambassador

Sports Star: Magic Johnson

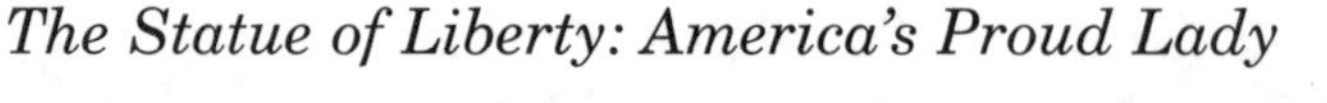

The Statue of Liberty: America's Proud Lady

Let's Meet...

David Hirsch has been a chef at Moosewood Restaurant in Ithaca, New York, for almost 20 years. Moosewood is a collectively run vegetarian eating establishment. David is also the author of *The Moosewood Restaurant Kitchen Garden.*

David Hirsch

Cookbook Author/Chef

How did you get started with Moosewood?

My desire to leave the city and join the back-to-the-land movement brought me to Ithaca in 1972. I got a job as a cook for some fraternities at Cornell University. I could have summers off and could devote time to other pursuits.

I discovered I loved to cook. It's fun and direct; the results are immediate. I got hooked up with Moosewood, by then in its third year, though at the time I wasn't thinking about a long-term career. I was disgruntled with cooking at the fraternities and wanted to be with people who shared my values. Moosewood was perfect.

What are your responsibilities at Moosewood?

I cook, plan meals, order food and supplies, test recipes for the books, write, attend meetings, and occasionally wait on tables.

Because of the success of our books, I go to local book signings, and do occasional television and radio shows. I also do some consulting and give presentations and cooking workshops.

What do you like most about your work?

From the very beginning I really liked Moosewood. It felt different to me from any other job. There's no hierarchy; you're working with peers.

The atmosphere is supportive, rather than competitive. You don't have a group of people vying for a vice presidency. There's a more honest approach on a daily basis. It's all very appealing, direct. You go in, make the food, and people appreciate it. I feel good about what I'm doing.

Another advantage working at Moosewood is that my duties can be varied. The days I am not in the kitchen on a cooking shift, I plan menus or write or test recipes for our forthcoming cookbooks.

Are there any downsides?

Dealing with the push and pull from all the different directions, the different people. Working with others towards agreement can be frustrating.

And as with any job, there is always some stress or concern. I was concerned about writing a whole book by myself. But I got a lot of support. Other Moosewood people helped out and tested my recipes. Writing requires a real commitment of time and space, and you always have deadlines hanging over your head.

Moosewood Restaurant House Dressing

In *The Moosewood Restaurant Kitchen Garden,* David tells us that this salad dressing changes with each meal and season. Each cook has a version. Here's David's:

- 1/4 cup loosely packed fresh parsley leaves
- 1/4 cup loosely packed fresh basil leaves (1 1/2 teaspoons dried)
- 3 tablespoons coarsely chopped scallion greens
- 1/2 teaspoon fresh lemon thyme leaves (1/4 teaspoon dried)
- 1/4 teaspoon freshly ground black pepper
- 1 teaspoon dijon mustard
- 1/2 cup milk
- 3 tablespoons cider vinegar
- 3 tablespoons water (or part apple juice for sweeter dressing)
- 1 cup vegetable oil (can be part olive)

Yields 2 Cups

In a blender, whirl all the ingredients, except the oil, for 1 minute. While the blender is running, slowly add the oil. Blend only until the dressing is thick and creamy.

The herbs can be varied to suit your taste, but maintain the proportions of liquid to oil for a creamy consistency.

Will keep refrigerated for up to a week.*

*Reprinted with permission from Simon & Schuster. Copyright 1992 by Vegetable Kingdom, Inc.

Not many writers reach the best-seller list in both fiction and nonfiction; but Tom Clancy, popular techno-thriller writer, did just that with his book, *Submarine: A Guided Tour Inside a Nuclear Warship*. A Berkley book, it had almost 372,000 copies in print after two printings.

How do you write, publish, and sell 3.6 million copies (and still counting) of a cookbook with healthful and tasty recipes? Become the personal cook for a well-known celebrity. That's what Oprah Winfrey's cook Rosie did. Oprah's photo on the book jacket, and a full show devoted to Rosie's recipes didn't hurt either. Publisher Knopf is having trouble keeping up with the demand. They literally can't print them fast enough.

Doubleday has managed a coup; they have signed a two-book contract with Anita Hill (for an undisclosed amount). One of the books issued in 1995 is Professor Hill's autobiography, which in her words, "will put the Senate hearings and my life in full and accurate perspective." Her second book will detail the historical roots of sexual harassment, the size of the present problem, and the possible remedies American citizens and the court system can put into effect.

Do you have an idea for a nonfiction book? If so, you should be able to answer Yes to these two questions before you begin writing.

1. Will your book be different, offering new or additional information, from all the similar books already published?
2. Will you be able to get the information you need to complete the book? Can your library help you with research materials, or are there experts you can locate and interview?

Here are the requirements of two publishing houses that publish nonfiction titles. Before making a submission to them, you should send an SASE and request their guidelines for writers.

The Globe Pequot Press publishes, on average, 70 books a year. They receive 1,500 submissions annually. The topics they are interested in include biography, carpentry, cookbooks, gardening, how-to, natural history, outdoor recreation, and travel guidebooks. You can submit an outline, a table of contents, and a sample chapter. They will also look at the completed manuscript. Write to Submissions Editor, Globe Pequot Press, P.O. Box 833, Old Saybrook, CT 06475.

Chronicle Books publishes an average of 100 titles per year. They receive 1,500 submissions annually. The topics they are interested in include coffee-table books, cookbooks, and regional California subjects covering art, design, gardening, health and medicine, nature, photography, recreation, and travel. Chronicle Books also publishes children's picture books, novels, and short story collections. Send a query letter or submit an outline with sample chapters for either nonfiction or fiction. Write to Executive Editor, Chronicle Books, 275 5th Street, San Francisco, CA 94103.

For more information the following books will help you.

How to Write a Book Proposal, by Michael Larsen, Writer's Digest Books, 1985.

How to Write and Sell Your First Nonfiction Book, by Oscar Collier with Frances Spatz Leighton (St. Martin's Press).

Other books by David Hirsch and the Moosewood Collective

Moosewood Restaurant Cooks at Home, by the Moosewood Collective, Simon & Schuster, 1994.

New Recipes From Moosewood Restaurant, by the Moosewood Collective, Ten Speed Press, 1987.

Freelance writers can find satisfying and financially rewarding work writing for others. Many people, business owners or politicians, for example, who either do not have the skill or the time to write, hire the services of professional writers.

You can keep busy writing magazine ads, travel brochures, political speeches, or press releases. The possibilities are as wide as the number of clients you can develop.

If you write well, have a good command of English grammar, and knowledge of or interest in a specialized subject, then a career writing for others might be for you.

When you write for others, you may work in your employer's office, or you may work from home, as a freelance writer.

You will meet with your client and listen to what he or she needs. Your project might be a brochure describing a resort hotel or a magazine ad to sell a new product.

You then estimate how long the job will take you, and what expenses, such as photography, you will have. Then give an exact price to the client. If your estimate was off and it takes you more time than you had initially planned, you still have to stick by your fee.

You most likely will be working on your own, and you must be self-motivated and disciplined. The client will want the project finished by a certain date and will expect you to deliver on time. That could mean you're working weekends and nights as well as days to get the job done.

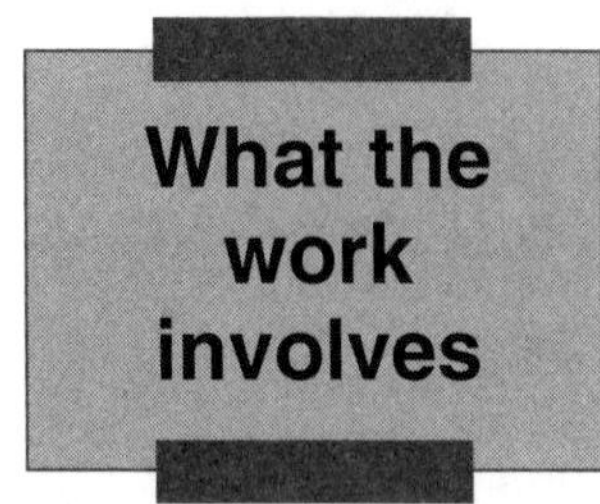

When you write for others, you could be involved in a variety of projects. Below is a selected list.

Advertising copywriters write all the words for magazine ads, and radio and TV commercials.

They also design and write brochures for businesses. They write all the copy for direct-mail packages, which are used to sell products or services through the mail.

Ghostwriters write books for people who don't have the necessary skill to do it themselves. The client could be a famous person—a former president or a movie star—who has a story to tell, but needs help doing it. Ghostwriters sometimes get credit for their writing, often they stay anonymous, writing behind the scenes.

Press secretaries work for government officials, actors, or big corporations that are concerned with relations with the press. They schedule public appearances and read prepared statements to reporters. They also write press releases, which are announcements of an event, service, or product. The press releases are sent to various newspapers and TV and radio shows to generate some free publicity.

Speech writers work with politicians and other public figures. listening to what they want to say, then writing the speeches they will deliver.

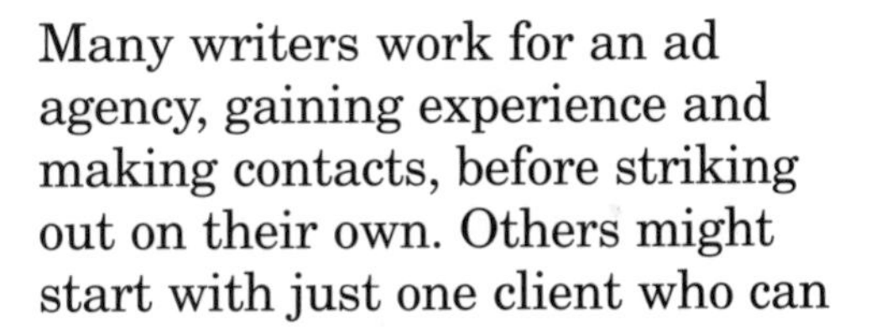

Many writers work for an ad agency, gaining experience and making contacts, before striking out on their own. Others might start with just one client who can send enough work their way. By building a reputation for being a good writer who delivers on time, you will be referred to new clients. Word-of-mouth is how most writers build up business.

Press secretary jobs are usually filled outside the civil service system; the members of congress hire directly. Knowing a congress-person is the best way to get a job, but most people don't. Others go to Washington (at their own expense) and walk the hallways of the House office building or the Senate, asking about openings.

Someone just out of college might try for an assistant press secretary position or volunteer time as a student intern.

Most writers are not particularly well paid. But in the case of writing for others, the money can be as rewarding as the work.

Most people who write for others do it on a freelance basis. Although some charge a flat hourly rate, most charge by the project. It can be feast or famine starting out, but once you build a steady client base, your income can be very attractive.

A few writers earn a straight salary as press secretaries and in advertising. Salaries in advertising range from $25,000 a year to $75,000 or more.

The chart below will tell you what freelancers charge for a few selected projects.

	Hourly	By the Project
Advertising copywriter	$20 to $100	$200 to $4,000
Book jacket copywriting		$100 to $600
Brochures	$20 to $50	$200 to $4,000
Business catalogs	$25 to $40	$60 to $75 per printed page
Direct-mail packages		$1,500 to $10,000
Encyclopedia articles		$60 to $80 per 1,000 words
Ghostwriting	$25 to $100	$400 to $25,000 or 100% of the advance and 50% of the royalties
Greeting cards		$20 to $200 per verse
Press release		$80 to $300
Speech writing	$20 to $75	$100 to $5,000
Technical writing	$35 to $75	$5 per page

Independence is one plus of writing for others, freelancers will tell you. Sometimes you can work in your home office, delivering the project when it's finished.

You choose the projects you want, and you set your own salary or fees.

The downside is that you have to learn to promote yourself and seek out clients, which sometimes means contacting strangers to offer your services.

Let's Meet...

Bob Mansker

Press Secretary

While working toward his degrees in business administration, Bob started volunteering for local political campaigns. Then Bob moved to Washington to serve as press secretary to Congressman Martin Frost, Democrat from Texas.

How did you get started?

I was always fascinated with reporters and politics—but didn't want to follow the traditional journalism track, working for newspapers or television and radio.

When I was involved with political campaigning and during a stint in the state legislature, I learned how to write press releases and newsletters for various members of Congress.

I met Congressman Frost in an earlier campaign I had volunteered for. We worked well together.

What does a congressional press secretary do?

I write press releases on the Congressman's position on a multitude of issues. These are sent to different media—newspapers, TV, radio—with the hopes the information will be printed or aired.

I also write a weekly newspaper column, and produce a monthly newsletter for the voters in the district. I produce radio and television programs, scheduling the Congressman in various studios. I also regularly meet with media representatives from various newspapers and magazines, television and radio.

About three or four times a year, I travel to and from the congressional district in Texas to remain acquainted with local media. And occasionally I get to travel abroad.

How can someone interested in your profession get started?

A college degree is not absolutely necessary. If someone understood the operation, had strong writing skills, and a knowledge of the home state, he or she could be hired. But, having the degree is usually an advantage. Practical experience campaigning is better than a degree in political science, however. But a major in general communications would be an advantage.

Writing, organizational abilities, and typing skills are crucial. And a good all-around press secretary needs some understanding of radio, television, and newspapers.

What do you enjoy most about your job?

I interact with people who are constantly keeping aware of national and world events and who respect the political process.

Also I get to bring my beagle, Vicky, to work. I have a new office that's out of the way a bit, and I'm the staff director, so no one minds.

What is the downside?

The job depends on the Congressman being re-elected and deciding to seek re-election.

Bob's Typical Day

9:00	Read office copy of *The Washington Post.*
9:20	Received press clippings from the congressional district in Texas, including the primary results.
9:30	Returned phone call to ABC correspondent.
10:00	Conference with Congressman regarding day's schedule.
10:30	Contacted television media representatives.
11:00	Worked on weekly column.
12:00	Lunch hour.
1:00	Conference with Congressman.
1:30	Set up interviews with television and newspaper reporters.
2:30	Accompanied Congressman to recording studio for taping of weekly report to district constituents.
3:30	Returned phone calls.
4:30	Checked news wire for events of the day.
5:00	Prepared press releases.
6:00	Exited office for home.

Let's Meet...

Rosalind has been writing advertising copy for brochures, magazine ads, and television commercials for more than 15 years. She feels that it's important to always meet your deadlines and to always give your clients their money's worth.

Rosalind Sedacca

Advertising Copywriter

What does an advertising copywriter do?

I write ads for magazines, TV and radio commercials, brochures, direct mail packages, video scripts, newsletters, sales letters, and any other material that a company needs to sell their product.

When you write an ad, the first thing you have to know is its purpose. Then you want to understand who will be eventually reading your writing. You have to understand the demographics—their age, sex, income, education, interests. If I'm writing a print ad for teenagers, I write it differently from an ad for mothers or engineers.

I work with graphic designers. I do the writing, and the graphic designers take care of the layout and art. We team up and brainstorm; the words alone don't work unless they're placed on the page in attractive ways.

How did you get started?

I got started out of college wanting to work for *Vogue* magazine in the editorial department. I went to their personnel department, but they didn't have any openings. Instead, they offered me a position in advertising, as an assistant to the woman who was writing subscription letters, offering subscriptions to the magazines.

A year later, she left the company, and I became creative director of circulation promotion for Conde Naste Publications, which owns *Vogue, Glamour, Mademoiselle, House and Garden,* and *Bride's.* It was a pretty cushy job for someone who was 21 years old. It made me a direct mail/advertising expert. I was with them for two years, then moved into more general advertising for various agencies. In 1984 I went out on my own, and I've been independent since then.

What do you like most about your work?

It's very stimulating and creative. I never get bored; no two days are ever the same. What I like best, and what also can be a challenge, is that one minute I'm writing about a hotel and the next minute I'm writing about a computer, and then I'm turning around and writing about a bank or about shoes. Sometimes it's hard to shift mental gears from one topic to another. It's the plus and the minus together.

But I've got a perfect mix. Part of the week I'm in my home office working at the computer. The other part of the week I'm at meetings, either getting new clients or delivering my work.

Tracking Counterfeiters

One of the most interesting projects Rosalind has ever worked on is a new invention designed to detect counterfeit products. Forgery has become an international crisis. Unsuspecting buyers, thinking they are purchasing real Rolex watches or Reebok shoes, for example, might end up with fakes. Counterfeiters also print fake tickets and fake money.

Rosalind's client invented a device that will help stop this problem. He has created a decoder that when placed over a plastic strip on the product will show if it's genuine or not. Manufacturers can travel to flea markets and shops to check for fake products. When the decoder is in place, they'll be able to read the words, "Genuine Reeboks" or "Genuine Currency."

Rosalind's job was to write a detailed brochure describing this new invention and to help set up a promotional tour. She arranged for her client to appear on "20/20" and other similar TV shows.

For Rosalind, subjects like this are the most fascinating part of her work.

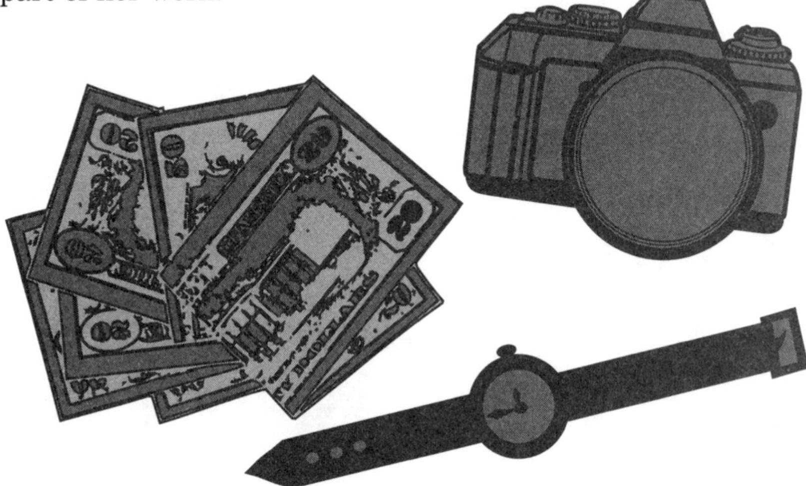

Robin Cook's *Fatal Cure* has become required reading for members of Congress. On the best-seller list with approximately 250,000 copies in print, the book covers the horrifying possibilities of a managed health care system. Senator Orrin Hatch, an opponent of President Bill Clinton's health care plan, recently suggested that Hilary Rodham Clinton read the book. Hatch's plan is also to distribute free copies to all members of Congress.

Super dog star Lassie went on a mini-book promotion tour, for an official *paw-o-graphing* of *Lassie: A Dog's Life, The First Fifty Years* (Penguin). S/he was accompanied by author Ace Collins.

Do you think you could provide clients with just the right words they're looking for? Here are three assignments for you. Why don't you give it a try?

Assignment #1: The mayor of your city wants to run for re-election. He has been invited to speak on a local television program. His audience will be voters who are concerned about crime in their neighborhood. He has about three minutes to speak and wants to win back the public's confidence in him. What speech would you write for him? After you've written the speech, try it out on your family and see their reaction.

Assignment #2: A possible client has a new product and wants a slogan for it. It's a soft drink your client claims tastes better than Coke and Pepsi. You have had a glass, and you agree. Without mentioning any of the competitors' brand names, what slogan would you write? (Here are a few examples of slogans: "The Pepsi

Generation," "Choosey mothers choose Jiff," "Fly the Friendly Skies of United.")

Assignment #3: You are a press secretary working for a best-selling author who is about to start on a book promotion tour to six major cities. He will be speaking about his book (*How To Get Rich Using Other People's Money*) and signing autographs at local bookstores. He has asked you to write a press release announcing the tour. The press release will be sent to the newspapers in each city. What five pieces of information are missing from your assignment to enable you to do the job properly?

(Answers: 1. The cities he will visit; 2. The dates of each stop on the tour; 3. The time of day he will speak; 4. The names and addresses of the bookstores at which he will speak; 5. The names and addresses of the newspapers you'll be sending the release to.)

The world of publishing is busy and exciting, filled with risks, and sometimes disappointments. Without publishers, writers would never see their words in print; there would be no magazines, newspapers, or books for the public to enjoy, no textbooks for students and teachers to use.

Publishing professionals wield a great deal of power. They determine what books and stories see print and help shape the tastes of the reading public.

In this chapter, meet a senior editor and literary agent, and learn what their jobs involve. Then you can decide on which side of the computer you'd prefer to work.

What agents and editors do

Literary agents act as go-betweens for writers and editors. Most of the large publishing houses refuse to consider manuscripts unless they are sent by an agent. Many publishers credit agents with the ability to screen out inappropriate submissions. An agent is expected to be familiar with the different kinds of books publishers prefer to take on.

An agent spends his or her time reading manuscripts, choosing which ones to work with, and then trying to sell them to publishers. Having an agent allows a writer to concentrate on writing instead of marketing. The agent's job is to find the right publisher for each client's work, and once successful, to negotiate the best financial deal for the writer. Agents also handle film rights for feature or TV movies, and foreign rights, selling books to publishers overseas.

Editors work in publishing houses or for magazines and newspapers. Editors read manuscripts, talk with writers, and decide which books or articles they will publish. Editors also have to read what other houses or publications are printing, to know what's out there and what's selling.

Once a manuscript is selected for publication, an editor oversees the various steps to produce the finished product, from line editing for mistakes, to the book or magazine cover art and copy.

Editors and agents also attend writer's conferences to speak to aspiring writers and to find new talent.

How publishing houses are structured

A small press that puts out only three or four books a year might operate with a staff of only two or three. Each person has to wear many hats: as acquisitions editor, finding new projects to publish; as typesetter and proofreader; as sales manager; as promoter and publicist; as clerk and secretary.

The large publishing houses, most of which are in New York City, can have more than 100 employees and are separated into different departments such as editorial, contracts, legal, sales and marketing, and publicity and promotion.

How literary agencies are structured

Some literary agents choose to work on their own, with little more than secretarial assistance. They rent space in an office building or work from a home office.

Other agents prefer to work within a literary agency, either as the owner, or as one of the associates. They can still function independently, choosing their own writers and book projects.

Usually in an agency, agents must contribute a percentage of their income to cover the office's operating expenses.

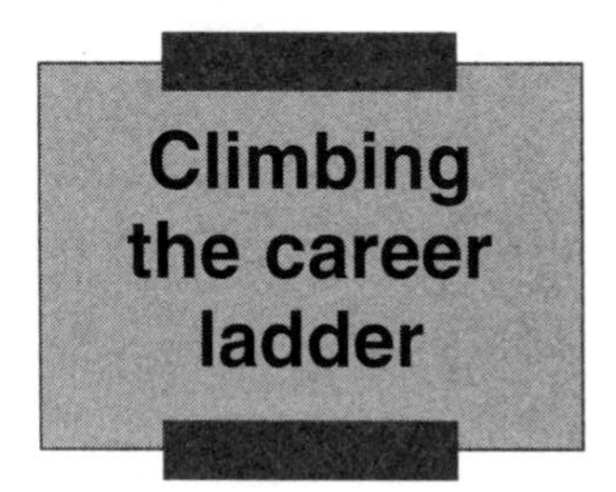

In publishing it's rare for someone to start out as an editor or agent without any prior experience. Many agents work for publishing houses first, becoming familiar with the editorial process and contracts, before moving into a literary agency.

And within a publishing house there is a distinct ladder most editors climb as they gain experience and develop a successful track record. They usually start out as editorial assistants, answering the phone, opening and distributing the mail, and typing correspondence. Some editorial assistants are first readers for their editors; they'll read a manuscript then write a reader's report. If it's a good report then the editor will take a look at the manuscript.

Most editorial assistants learn the editing process from the editor they work for, and over time move up into editorial positions with more and more responsibility.

Most editors and agents have at least a bachelor's degree, although not necessarily in English. Any liberal arts or humanities major, in addition to writing and literature courses, will provide the necessary

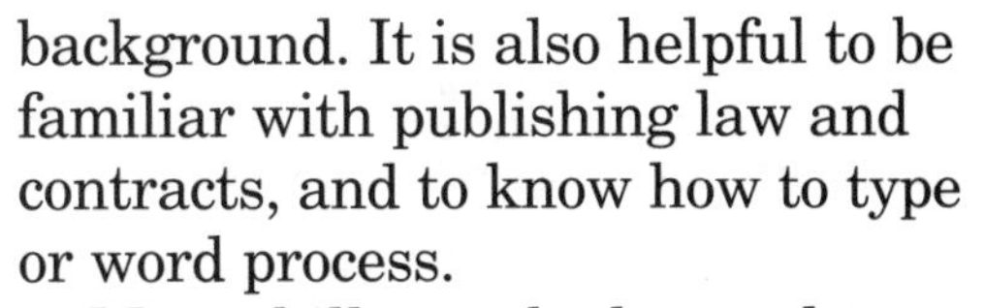

background. It is also helpful to be familiar with publishing law and contracts, and to know how to type or word process.

Most skills can be learned on the job, but, as with writers, editors and agents should also be avid readers.

Editors are generally paid a set salary. Although their weekly salary does not depend on the sales of the books they choose to publish, an editor with a good track record is likely to be promoted and given raises. Starting pay, however, is not glamorous.

Agents, on the other hand, must sell their clients' manuscripts to publishers in order to earn any income. Agents generally work on a commission basis, 10 to 15 percent of the money the writer earns. If an agent knows the market, carefully chooses manuscripts, and has success bargaining for big advances and royalty percentages, then he or she can make a very good living, often much more than the editors to whom he or she is selling.

In a bad year, however, an agent can often have to struggle to make a living.

Let's Meet...

Nancy Yost

Literary Agent

Nancy Yost started out as a contract editor at Random House, then worked as an editor at Avon Books. Now she is one of three full-time agents at Lowenstein Associates, Inc., in New York City who, together, represent more than 150 writers.

Why did you decide to switch roles from editor to agent?

Publishing houses are organized by lists—certain kinds of books they're good at, and certain books they don't do. For example, Avon is very good with romances and original mysteries; they have great science fiction and fantasy editors. But if you ever wanted to work with a big picture book or a cookbook, you couldn't. It seemed to me that if I became an agent I'd be able to play in everyone's backyard instead of just one.

And the money is better, of course; the more you sell, the more you earn. And you only work with the people you want to work with. Even in the best of publishing houses you have marketing and production people who many times disagree with your enthusiasm for a book. The only limit now is what I think the market can do. If one publisher doesn't like it, I can go to six others—or twenty others—until I sell it or until I realize I'm not going to be able to sell it.

Tell us about your job.

It's very busy. I carry 50 clients at any one time. That's not to say I am always trying to sell 50 new manuscripts at once. Each of my writers produces one to two books a year, and my time is easily manageable.

I like to work with narrative nonfiction—true crime, science books, human interest stories, offbeat humor titles—and commercial fiction including contemporary women's novels and mysteries.

I receive a lot of submissions every week—query letters and complete manuscripts. I use a triage approach to my submissions. The ones that are going to die, I reject right away; the ones that I'm really excited about, I ask to see more right away. The ones that have some potential but don't really stand out, tend to sit the longest. Some really good manuscripts sit for a long time, too, when I'm too busy with other commitments.

Once I have received a presentable manuscript, I talk to editors on the phone before I send them out. It gives me a chance to feel them out, and to express my enthusiasm for the project.

What are some of the upsides to your job?

I'm always excited when a manuscript comes in that has quality—style, voice, fresh thinking. But a manuscript needing a lot of editing won't interest me. It won't be worth my while to take something like that on unless it's perfectly fabulous, and I can see major money for it.

And, of course, making the sale is an up.

Nancy's Trek Through the Slush Pile

Nancy had just come to the agency from her job as editor at Avon Books, and she had no clients and no work to do.

"The first week I spent reading unsolicited manuscripts from morning to night. They had been in a dust-covered pile for six months because no one had time to read them. I found a manuscript that completely riveted me the minute I started reading it. There's that spark of recognition you get when something is really good.

"Then of course there was the fear that the author had already agreed to work with another agent, but when I called her and told her how much I liked her manuscript she said no one had done anything yet.

"We reworked it a little, and within two weeks of my new job I made a five-figure sale for the author.

"When it was in the slush pile, it was called *Like A Shadow, Like A Dream.* It's about a woman who moves into a Boston townhouse that appears to be haunted. You might know it better as *Shattered Echoes,* by Barbara Shapiro."

Let's Meet...

John Scognamiglio (both g's are silent) joined Zebra books as a senior editor in 1992. He is also a published author with two contemporary women's novels to his credit.

John Scognamiglio

Senior Editor

What are your duties as senior editor?

I handle historical romance, horror, mystery, suspense, women-in-jeopardy, young adult horror, women's mainstream fiction, and contemporary romance. I read manuscripts, confer with authors, do the line editing, write cover copy, go to conferences to meet with aspiring writers, and have lunch with agents.

I also do a lot of coordination with all the different departments within the publishing house: publicity, promotion, sales. And then there are the meetings. Publishing houses usually work about nine months ahead, so in a marketing meeting we discuss books that are coming out in the next year.

We also have editorial meetings to bring up new projects. We discuss the book and the author's history. The editor would usually get the go-ahead from the editor in chief. If it's a go, then there's negotiation over the financial terms with the agent, or with the author directly.

What do you like most about being an editor?

I love the whole editorial process from beginning to end and knowing that once your work is done you have a finished product, a book. I like working with authors and watching them grow from book to book. I can point out their strengths and weaknesses; I want to help make my authors succeed, not only for their sake, but for mine, because it shows that I'm doing a good job.

When I'm working with submissions, I get excited seeing stories where the characters really come to life. I like a writer who knows how to develop the story and knows where it's going. They're not rushing through their story.

And I like receiving submissions from writers who have done their homework. They know what kind of books we publish. I don't like receiving something that clearly is not a Zebra book.

And also, I think that most people go into editing because they love to read. It's true for me. I love books.

Are there any downsides?

Only that I never have enough time to do my own personal reading. I'm always reading manuscripts or proposals. I have to budget my time for pleasure reading. And I don't particularly like line editing; that's grunt work.

How can someone get started?

Take any sort of job that will get your foot in the door. I always wanted to be an editor. I started out as a contract assistant, became an assistant to the magazine editor, and then I became an editorial assistant.

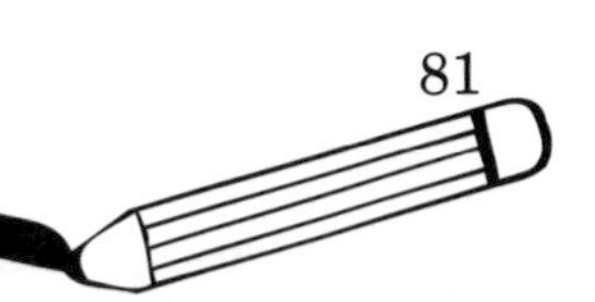

Two Exciting "Firsts"

The first exciting moment for John was holding the first book he'd ever edited, once it was all finished and off the presses. It was called a *Delicate Matter* by Rebecca Forster, and it was about a young woman and her life in Hollywood in the 1940s.

"It had been one of my boss's projects; she passed it on to me, and it was the first book I got to work on. I was an editorial assistant at the time. I did the line editing, and I got to talk with the author about ideas for the cover. I enjoyed working with her—she's still one of my authors today. I remember walking into a bookstore and seeing it on a shelf. That was particularly exciting.

"The other moment was when one of my authors thanked me in print in the acknowledgments in the book, recognizing my work. That's always very special when an author does that."

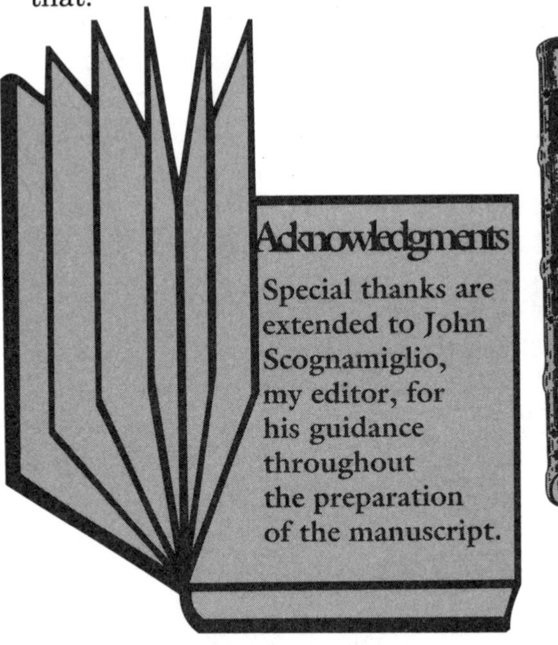

The Celestine Prophecy, a best-seller by James Redfield, was originally self-published. The novel is about an ancient manuscript that explains the meaning of life. Bookstores have reported unusually high turnouts for Redfield's personal appearances. An average of 400 people show up at bookstores to buy a signed copy of his book. At one lecture he attracted 1,400 readers.

The team of Felecia Hudson and husband, Elliot Shaw, writing as "Felecia Elliot," received an advance of $250,000 for their first novel, *The Trusted.* It's a tale of intrigue and adventure involving a Palm Beach billionaire. But how did this American couple wind up with a British publisher? Elliot was in the British Virgin Islands and met the senior editor there. He asked him to take a look . . . and the rest is history. *The Trusted* had been turned down by several U.S. publishers first.

To find out if a career in publishing is right for you take this mini-quiz. Don't look at the answers until you are finished.

1. You are a senior editor of fiction, and there are three manuscripts sitting on your desk. Your problem is that you can publish only one of them. Which one do you think will be a bestseller?
   A. A sappy love story about a couple who has only a short time together and then never sees each other again.
   B. A sappy love story about a couple from different backgrounds. They marry but shortly afterward the wife dies.
   C. A moving and funny love story about a woman who has been unlucky in love. She meets a wonderful man who wants to marry her, but she turns him down without realizing he's an angel sent from heaven to make her happy.
2. You are a literary agent, and you have three authors who want you to represent them.

Your problem is that you have room on your list for only one more client. Which writer do you take on?

A. This writer has never been published before. His book is about a young girl who kills everyone at the senior prom.

B. This writer has had three successful books published and wants to find a new agent. But his fourth book, the one you are considering, is poorly plotted and slow reading. The author refuses to revise his book.

C. This writer's first book had very slow sales. His second book is sitting on your desk. It's about a young lawyer who accepts a job in a small southern law firm.

1. A and B were both bestsellers: Robert Waller's *The Bridges of Madison County* and Erich Segal's *Love Story*. C has not been published yet. Go figure.
2. Most agents would probably choose B, feeling it's safer to go with an established writer. But A is Stephen King's first book, *Carrie,* and C is John Grisham's *The Firm.* Go figure.

INDEX